THE
267
STUPIDEST
THINGS
Democrats
EVER SAID

BY
TED RUETER

THREE RIVERS PRESS
NEW YORK

Copyright © 2000 by Ted Rueter

Published by Three Rivers Press, New York, New York. Member of the Crown Publishing Group.

Random House, Inc. New York, Toronto, London, Sydney, Auckland
www.randomhouse.com

THREE RIVERS PRESS is a registered trademark and the Three Rivers Press colophon is a trademark of Random House, Inc.

Printed in the United States of America

Designed by Susan Maksuta

Library of Congress Cataloging-in-Publication Data
Rueter, Ted.
The 267 stupidest things Republicans have ever said—the 267 stupidest things Democrats have ever said / by Ted Rueter—1st ed.
          p.   cm.
1. United States—Politics and government—1945–1989—Humor. 2. United States—Politics and government—1989—Humor. 3. United States—Politics and government—1945–1989—Quotations, maxims, etc. 4. United States—Politics and government—1989—Quotations, maxims, etc. 5. Politicians—United States—Quotations. 6. Politicians—United States—Humor. 7. Republican Party (U.S. : 1854–)—Humor. 8.Democratic Party (U.S.)—Humor. 9. American wit and humor. I. Title.
E838.3 .R84 2000
973.92'02'07—dc21   99-59995

ISBN 0-609-80635-1

10 9 8 7

First Edition

Achievement

"We shall reach greater and greater platitudes of achievement."
—Richard J. Daley (mayor of Chicago, 1955–1976)

Actors

"If President Reagan could be an actor and become president, maybe I could become an actor. I've got a good pension. I can work for cheap."
—Bill Clinton, at a Hollywood fund-raiser

African-Americans

"I look like you."
—Lawrence Bell (candidate for mayor of Baltimore, 1999), telling a black crowd why they should vote for him

"The first black president will be a politician who is black."
—Doug Wilder (governor of Virginia, 1989–1993). Wilder, who is black, briefly sought the Democratic presidential nomination in 1992.

Air Force One

"I may be the only person who's flown on both Air Force One and Con Air."

> —*Webster Hubbell (assistant attorney general, 1993–1994), to the American Bar Association convention. Hubbell spent eighteen months in jail for mail and tax fraud.*

Alone

"It depends on how you define *alone* . . ."

> —*Bill Clinton, in his grand jury testimony on the Monica Lewinsky affair*

"There were a lot of times when we were alone, but I never really thought we were."

> —*Bill Clinton, elaborating on the nuances of "alone" for the grand jury*

American Society

"I thought it was a significant development for American society."

> —*Jim Wright (Speaker, U.S. House of Representatives, 1986–1989), on why he placed a plug in* The Congressional Record *for a motivational video by a company that paid his wife $36,000 a year*

Amtrak Service

"I share your view that the urgent problems of species extinction and the conservation of biological diversity should be addressed. The first step in saving any plant or animal from extinction is to become aware of and respect the fragile ecosystems that make up our own planet."

—*Al Gore, answering a letter from a Dallas couple who complained that Amtrak service cuts were eliminating the "Texas Eagle" connecting Dallas to the West Coast and Chicago*

Assault

"His boss may have needed choking. It may have been justified. . . . Someone should have asked the question, 'What prompted that?'"

—*Willie Brown (mayor of San Francisco, 1996–), defending Latrell Sprewell of the Golden State Warriors for choking and threatening to kill his coach. Brown also said, "This is not a person accused of rape, accused of kicking a TV cameraman, accused of carrying a gun on an airplane."*

Bagels

"At breakfast, she was complaining that it is impossible to get a decent bagel in Washington."

—*Bill Clinton, on Hillary's run for the U.S. Senate from New York*

Marion Barry

"At no time did I see any drugs, use any drugs, or have any knowledge of drugs. It would be inconsistent with my character, with my integrity, with my veracity, to be involved in such activity or to be around such persons who would knowingly do this."

> —*Marion Barry (former mayor of Washington, D.C.). Barry made this statement in January 1989, after he was arrested for cocaine possession in an FBI sting operation.*

"I am a great mayor. I am an upstanding Christian man. I am an intelligent man. I am a deeply educated man. I am a humble man."

> —*Marion Barry*

Baywatch

"I feel like I'm on *Baywatch*."

> —*Hillary Rodham Clinton, surrounded by lifeguards on a Long Island beach during her New York State "listening tour."*

Beverly Hills

"Ever feel like politicians in Washington, D.C., don't care what people in Beverly Hills, California, think?"

> —*Robert Torricelli (senator from New Jersey, 1997–), in a 1999 fund-raising letter.*

Bilingualism

"You know, back home, Bubba thinks we ought to just speak English in this country."

> —*Wallace Wilkinson (governor of Kentucky, 1987–1991), commenting on the bilingualism of 1988 Democratic presidential nominee Michael Dukakis*

Birth

"No, Mr. Chancellor, I was born in a manger."

> —*Lyndon Johnson (president, 1963–1969), responding to West German chancellor Ludwig Erhard, who said, "I understand you were born in a log cabin, Mr. President."*

Blackness

"I went out and bought some Berlitz tapes . . . I'm practicing my pronunciation of 'Yo.'"

> —*Anthony Williams (mayor of Washington, D.C., 1998–), defending himself against charges that he wasn't "black enough"*

George Bush

"People would say, 'We need a man on the ticket.'"

> —*Pat Schroeder (representative from Colorado, 1973–1996), on why George Bush was unlikely to choose a woman as his running mate in 1988*

George W. Bush

"We crossed paths. Are there pictures of us dancing on a bar together? No. I don't have that."

> —*John Kerry (senator from Massachusetts, 1985–), on his run-ins with George W. Bush, a Yale classmate*

Campaigning

"I don't want to go around shaking hands and having babies pee on me."

> —*Barbra Streisand (Democratic political activist), on why she has no plans to run for public office*

Candidates

"We've got a strong candidate. I'm trying to think of his name."

> —*Christopher Dodd (senator from Connecticut, 1981–), referring to Elliot Close, a candidate for the U.S. Senate from South Carolina against Strom Thurmond. At the time, Dodd was cochairman of the Democratic National Committee.*

Cattle Futures

"I was lucky."

> —*Hillary Rodham Clinton, explaining how she transformed a $1,000 investment into a $100,000 payoff. More likely, she was the beneficiary of a money-transfer scheme.*

Cemeteries

"Being president is like running a cemetery: You've got a lot of people under you, and nobody's listening."
> —*Bill Clinton*

Charity

"Charity is taking an ugly girl to lunch."
> —*Warren Beatty (Democratic party activist)*

Charts

"The chart you had was very moving."
> —*Bill Clinton, at his Little Rock economic summit in December 1992, responding to a chart concerning wage disparities between high school graduates and college graduates*

Check Bouncing

"They gave me a book of checks. They didn't ask for any deposits."
> —*Joe Early (representative from Massachusetts, 1975–1982), at a 1982 press conference concerning the House check-bouncing scandal*

"It's not like molesting young girls or young boys. It's not a show-stopper."
> —*Charlie Wilson (representative from Texas, 1973–1996), on his eighty-one bounced checks*

Childhood Memories

"It is among the first memories I have of the government of the United States, and probably the first hearing of the United States Senate I ever witnessed. It was only a flickering television screen, but I will never forget it, and even if I tried, my family will never allow me."

> —*Bob Torricelli (senator from New Jersey, 1997–), on the Senate hearings on organized crime, led by Senator Estes Kefauver. Torricelli was born on August 26, 1951; the Kefauver hearings ended five days later.*

Bill Clinton

"Yes, Bill Clinton is a big flirt. He flirts with me. He flirts with women. He flirts with pets."

> —*Dee Dee Myers (press secretary to President Clinton, 1993–1994)*

"I've got to be more like John Wayne."

> —*Bill Clinton, agreeing with David Gergen, his new advisor, that he needed to appear more "presidential"*

"Give Bill a second term, and Al Gore and I will be turned loose to do what we really want to do."

> —*Hillary Rodham Clinton, campaigning in 1996*

"Hell, if you work for Bill Clinton, you go up and down more times than a whore's nightgown."

> —*James Carville (Democratic political consultant)*

"I like Bill Clinton. Do I think he's a total idiot? Yes."

> —*Harold Ickes (former deputy chief of staff, Clinton White House)*

Hillary Rodham Clinton

"I think in the very near future the President will be known as your husband."

> —*Dan Rostenkowski (representative from Illinois, 1959–1994). In 1993, Rostenkowski was the chairman of the House Ways and Means Committee. He made this statement after Hillary testified on health care.*

"'You're too old, you can't see, and you're a woman. Maybe the dogs would take you.'"

> —*Hillary Rodham Clinton, recounting how a Marine recruiter rejected her application in 1975, when she was twenty-seven. "Dogs" refers to the Army.*

Clothing

"I tell you, he isn't wearing anything when we go to bed."

> —*Tipper Gore, defending her husband against charges that he paid journalist Naomi Wolf $15,000 a month to advise him how to dress like an "alpha male" rather than a "beta male"*

Cocaine

"At least when I was governor, cocaine was expensive."

—Jerry Brown (governor of California, 1975–1982)

Colored Handkerchiefs

"Rather than take a chance of being embarrassed again, I'm going to start buying colored handkerchiefs."

—Howell Heflin (senator from Alabama, 1979–1996), after pulling a pair of his wife's panties out of his pocket

Condoms

"If I could be the condom queen and get every young person in the United States who is engaging in sex to use a condom, I would wear a crown on my head with a condom on it."

—Joycelyn Elders (surgeon general, 1993–1994)

Congress

"No, but it can be rented."

—John Breaux (senator from Louisiana, 1987–), asked if his Senate vote could be bought

"He's trying to take the decision out of the hands of twelve honest men and give it to 435 congressmen!"

> —*Charles Vanik (representative from Ohio, 1959–1994), upon hearing that Vice President Spiro Agnew, indicted for bribery, wanted to have his case heard by the U.S. House of Representatives rather than a court of law*

"I'm always impressed by your disdain of Congress. That's one of the reasons you have such good relations with us."

> —*Joe Biden (senator from Delaware, 1973–), to Attorney General Ed Meese*

"What right does Congress have to go around making laws just because they deem it necessary?"

> —*Marion Barry (former mayor of Washington, D.C.)*

Consumers

"Honest businessmen should be protected from the unscrupulous consumer."

> —*Lester Maddox (governor of Georgia, 1967–1971), explaining why Georgia should not create a consumer protection agency*

Contrition

"What is with you reporters about contrition? I mean, what do you want? Do you want someone to walk around with a crying towel?"

—Dan Rostenkowski (representative from Illinois, 1959–1974),
after serving thirteen months in prison for mail fraud

Crime

"Outside of the killings, Washington has one of the lowest crime rates in the country."

—Marion Barry (former mayor of Washington, D.C.)

"I haven't committed a crime. What I did was fail to comply with the law."

—David Dinkins (mayor of New York, 1991–1994), answering
accusations that he failed to pay his taxes

Criticism

"They have slandered me, they have castigated me, they have vilified me, yes, they have even criticized me."

—Richard J. Daley (mayor of Chicago, 1955–1976)

Decisiveness

"I'm not indecisive. Am I indecisive?"

> —*Jim Scheibel (mayor of St. Paul, Minnesota, 1990–1993)*

"I guess I would have voted with the majority if it was a close vote. But I agree with the arguments the minority made."

> —*Bill Clinton, asked in January 1991 how he would have voted on the congressional resolution authorizing President Bush to go to war in the Persian Gulf*

Democrats

"Democrats did very well in Democratic primaries."

> —*Dee Dee Myers (press secretary to President Clinton, 1993–1994)*

Desire

"I desire you."

> —*Jimmy Carter (president, 1977–1981), referring to the Polish people. This was a translator's interpretation of Carter's statement that he "desired" to be in Poland.*

Differences

"Differences between me and President Clinton? That's a very thin file. Let me pull it out here. Wait a minute. Nothing seems to be in it."

> —*Al Gore*

Disasters

"This is the worst disaster in California since I was elected."

> —*Pat Brown (governor of California, 1959–1966), discussing a flood*

Draft

"The only way we'll ever get a volunteer army is to draft 'em."

> —*F. Edward Hebert (representative from Louisiana, 1941–1976)*

Drilling

"I had a drill to the tooth of America for the last two years."

> —*Bill Clinton in 1995, likening his politically unpopular actions to visits to the dentist*

"Well, Teddy: I see you've changed your position on offshore drilling."

> —*Howell Heflin (senator from Alabama, 1969–1996), looking at a picture of Ted Kennedy engaging in sexual activities with a woman on a boat*

"Now that I'm a homeowner, I better get one of these. I've never seen one before."

> —*Bill Clinton, referring to a cordless power drill*

"If ignorance ever goes to forty dollars a barrel, I want drilling rights on George Bush's head."

> —*Jim Hightower (Texas Commissioner of Agriculture, 1983–1990)*

Drunken Irishmen

"Every time they make an agreement, they're like a couple of drunks walking out of the bar for the last time. When they get to the swinging door, they turn right around and go back. They turn right around and go back in and say, 'I just can't quite get there.'"

> —*Bill Clinton, on peace negotiations in Ireland. He apologized the next day.*

E Pluribus Unum

"*E pluribus unum.* Out of one, many."

> —*Al Gore on ethnic diversity in Milwaukee, misquoting a phrase that actually means the opposite: Out of many, one.*

Egomania

"Whenever I speak, it's prime time."

> —*Jesse Jackson, (1988 presidential candidate), on why it didn't matter that he was not given a prime-time speaking slot at the 1996 Democratic National Convention*

Elderly

"Old people have a duty to die and get out of the way."

> —*Richard Lamm (governor of Colorado, 1975–1987)*

Emotional Attachments

"I'm someone who has a deep emotional attachment to *Starsky and Hutch.*"

> —*Bill Clinton*

Endorsements

"I endorse him! I endorse him! I endorse him! There, three times I endorsed him."

> —*Mario Cuomo (governor of New York, 1983–1994), asked about his bland endorsement of Michael Dukakis's presidential campaign in 1988*

Enemies

"Maybe some of it is people don't like my hairstyle."

> —*Hillary Rodham Clinton, explaining how she made so many political enemies*

Español

"Machismo gracias."

> —*Al Gore, visiting a school in a Hispanic portion of Albuquerque, New Mexico, during the 1996 presidential campaign. At the beginning of his speech, Gore was supposed to say "muchas gracias" ("many thanks"). Instead, he said "machismo gracias," which means "manliness thanks."*

Evolution

"All the ills from which America suffers can be traced back to the teaching of evolution. It would be better to destroy every other book ever written and save just the first three verses of Genesis."

> —*William Jennings Bryan (1924 Democratic presidential nominee)*

Executive Orders

"Stroke of the pen. Law of the land. Kinda cool."

> —*Paul Begala (Democratic political consultant), on President Clinton's use of executive orders*

Experience

"I don't see what's wrong with giving Bobby a little experience before he starts to practice law."

> —*John Kennedy, reacting to critics who argued that Robert Kennedy was too young to be attorney general*

"I have the experience to be governor. I know how to play craps. I know how to get in and out of the Baptist Church and ride horses. I know the oil and gas business. I know both sides of the streets."

> —*Earl Long (governor of Louisiana, 1939–1940, 1949–1953, 1957–1960)*

Family Values

"I really haven't talked to him about that."

> —*Hillary Rodham Clinton, asked whether her husband would live with her in their new house in Chappaqua, New York*

Famous Last Words

"Follow me around. I don't care. I'm serious. If anybody wants to put a tail on me, go ahead. They'd be very bored."

> —*Gary Hart (senator from Colorado, 1975–1986). Tom Fiedler of the* Miami Herald *took Hart up on his offer. He staked out Hart's D.C. town house, and saw that Donna Rice was an overnight guest.*

Fire Hydrants

"Sometimes I feel like the fire hydrant looking at a pack of dogs. For six years I have declined to tell those kinds of jokes, because I have been told it is not presidential. But I feel kind of outdoorsy today."

> —*Bill Clinton, at a party honoring the 150th anniversary of the Interior Department*

Steve Forbes

"He looked like he was the college president of the University of Mars."

> —*Paul Begala (Democratic political consultant)*

Gerald Ford

"Gerald Ford is a nice guy, but he played too much football with his helmet off."

> —*Lyndon Johnson (president, 1963–1969)*

Foreign Leaders

"George Bush has met more heads of foreign states than I have. But a substantial number of them were dead."

> —*Jesse Jackson (1988 Democratic presidential candidate)*

Foreign Policy

"China gets $60 billion in MFN status from Uncle Sam. Russia gets $15 billion in foreign aid from Uncle Sam. In exchange, Uncle Sam gets nuclear missiles pointed at our cities, two tape decks, and three cases of vodka. Beam me up. I say our national security brain trust needs a proctologist on staff."

—James Traficant (representative from Ohio, 1985–)

Friendship

"We have been boyhood friends all of our lives."
—Richard J. Daley (mayor of Chicago, 1955–1976)

"I had [two messages]. One was the White House and President Clinton. One was a former drug dealer that I represented, both congratulating me. So I said, 'That says it all.'"

—Oscar Goodman (mayor of Las Vegas, 1999–) on his election-night experiences. Goodman made his name as an attorney representing accused mobsters.

Fuzziness

"We're all fuzzy on the issues. The advantage of being a presidential candidate is you have a much broader range of issues on which to be fuzzy."

—Jimmy Carter (president, 1977–1981), on why he felt a kinship with successful congressional candidates

Gender

"People get a male candidate and you know right away what to do to make him look busy. Undo the collar, undo the tie, take off their coats. What does a woman do? We either look like an unmade bed or we look like a *Vogue* model."

> —*Pat Schroeder (representative from Colorado, 1973–1996)*

"Bill Clinton should wake up every single morning and thank the Lord for women."

> —*Mike McCurry (press secretary to President Clinton, 1994–1998), referring to Clinton's favorability ratings among women voters*

Gentleman

"Parliamentary question, Mr. Chairman: Do we have to call the gentleman a gentleman when he is not?"

> —*Pat Schroeder (representative from Colorado, 1973–1996), after California Republican Randy Cunningham used the phrase "homos in the military" during a House debate*

Newt Gingrich

"Maybe we can send him some of those little M&M's with the presidential seal on them."

> —*Mike McCurry (press secretary to President Clinton, 1994–1998), responding to Newt Gingrich's complaint that he was forced to exit Air Force One from the back*

Al Gore

"People who didn't know me well thought I was frozen stiff."

> *—Al Gore, on venturing outside during a cold snap in Washington, D.C., in 1996*

"I have told him to go out and have a good time."

> *—Bill Clinton, describing his political advice to Vice President Gore*

"I asked him to do it because he was the only person that I could trust to read all 150,000 pages in the *Code of Federal Regulations*."

> *—Bill Clinton, explaining why he chose Vice President Gore to be in charge of reforming the federal government*

Gratitude

"I want to thank each and every one of you for having extinguished yourselves this session."

> *—Gib Lewis (Speaker, Texas House of Representatives, 1983–1993)*

"I cannot tell you how grateful I am. I am filled with humidity."

> *—Gib Lewis, after having been reelected Speaker at the end of a legislative session*

Great Society

"There's a meritorious spot for all good men like you in the Great Society. The Great Society is going to be right expensive. I'll appoint you a taxpayer of the Great Society."

> —*Hubert Humphrey (vice president, 1965–1969). Humphrey was speaking to the North Carolina Farmers Council in Raleigh. A member of the audience said he was too old for Head Start and too young for Medicare, and thus didn't know where he fit in the Great Society.*

Handouts

"People don't want handouts! People want hand jobs!"

> —*William O'Neill (governor of Connecticut, 1980–1991), at a campaign rally. The crowd erupted into boisterous applause.*

Happiness

"She's a wonderful, wonderful person, and we're looking to a happy and wonderful night—ah, life."

> —*Ted Kennedy (senator from Massachusetts, 1963–), on his then fiancée, Victoria Reggie*

Helicopters

"They're *all* my helicopters, son."

> —*Lyndon Johnson (president, 1963–1969), to an Air Force corporal who pointed out the presidential helicopter, saying, "This is your helicopter, sir."*

History

"What's a man got to do to get in the top fifty?"

> —*Bill Clinton, after a survey of journalists ranked the Monica scandal the fifty-third most significant story of the century*

"This is unparalyzed in the state's history."

> —*Gib Lewis (Speaker, Texas House of Representatives, 1983–1993)*

Hospitality

"I thought you were real people."

> —*Hillary Rodham Clinton, after withdrawing an invitation to spectators to attend a reception for Supreme Court Justice Ruth Badar Ginsburg when she found out they were reporters*

Hubert Humphrey

"I am speaking of a great man who should have been president and would have been one of the greatest presidents in history: Hubert Horatio Hornblower."

>—*Jimmy Carter (president, 1977–1981), during his acceptance speech at the 1980 Democratic National Convention. Reportedly, this is what Carter called Humphrey behind closed doors.*

"He has Minnesota running-water disease. I've never known anyone from Minnesota that could keep their mouth shut. It's just something in the water out there."

>—*Lyndon Johnson (president, 1963–1969), on his vice president, Hubert Humphrey*

Idealism

"I say get 'em by the balls and their hearts and minds will follow."

>—*Mendel Rivers (representative from South Carolina, 1941–1970), during a debate over the best method to win the hearts and minds of foreign nations*

Illegal Campaign Fund-raising

"I didn't realize I was in a Buddhist temple."

>—*Al Gore, responding to questions about illegal fund-raising that took place in a Buddhist temple in Los Angeles in 1996*

Impeachment

"Not bad."

> —*Bill Clinton, asked how it felt to have been impeached*

Imprisonment

"If we could get every public official in prison for a few months, the policy would change greatly."

> —*Webster Hubbell (assistant attorney general, 1993–1994),*
> *meeting with the Families Against Mandatory Minimums*

Inhaling

"When I was in England, I experimented with marijuana a time or two, and I didn't like it. I didn't inhale and never tried it again."

> —*Bill Clinton, during the 1992 presidential campaign*

"Sure, if I could. I tried before."

> —*Bill Clinton, in response to the question, "If you had to do it*
> *over again, would you inhale?"*

Intergalactic Tourism

"Most people, when they look to the skies, see friend or foe. Not me. I see intergalactic tourists."

> —*Bob Miller (governor of Nevada, 1991–1998), dedicating a*
> *ninety-eight-mile stretch of road near a secret Air Force base.*
> *Miller dubbed it the "Extraterrestrial Highway."*

Internet

"During my service in the U.S. Congress, I took the initiative in creating the Internet."

> —*Al Gore, explaining why Democrats should support him over Bill Bradley for the 2000 presidential nomination*

Ireland

"No man is an Ireland."

> —*Richard J. Daley (mayor of Chicago, 1955–1976)*

Is

"It depends on what the meaning of the word *is* is."

> —*Bill Clinton, during his 1998 grand jury testimony on the Monica Lewinsky affair*

Issues

"There are no issues. My opponent has a job and I want it. That's what this election is about."

> —*William Bulow (governor of South Dakota, 1927–1931)*

Italian Men

"You people married Italian men. You know what it's like."

> —*Geraldine Ferraro (representative from New York, 1979–1984), attempting to explain why she hadn't been able to convince her husband, John Zaccaro, to release his financial records*

Jesse Jackson

"Jesse don't wanna run nothing but his mouth."

> —*Marion Barry (former mayor of Washington, D.C.), when told that Jesse Jackson was considering running against him for mayor of Washington, D.C.*

Michael Jackson

"The music of you and your brothers has been an inspiration to millions."

> —*Ted Kennedy (senator from Massachusetts, 1963–), to Michael Jackson, a white, middle-aged radio talk-show host in Los Angeles*

JFK

"He won't have a chance. I hate to see him and Bobby work themselves to death and lose."

> —*Joseph P. Kennedy (U.S. Ambassador to the United Kingdom) on why his son, John F. Kennedy, shouldn't run for president*

Job References

"I'm praying, of course, that Hillary will win. If she doesn't— Lord, I'll have to call Revlon again."

> —*Vernon Jordan (advisor to Bill Clinton), referring to Hillary Rodham Clinton's bid for a New York Senate seat. Jordan had called Revlon to help Monica Lewinsky get a job.*

Johnson Treatment

"If you say no, I'll have you drafted."

> —*Lyndon Johnson (president, 1963–1969), attempting to convince Georgia Senator Richard Russell to become a member of the Warren Commission on the assassination of President Kennedy. Russell accepted the offer.*

Paula Jones

"She has that 'come hither' look."

> —*Bill Clinton, to Danny Ferguson, an Arkansas state trooper, on May 8, 1991, at the Excelsior Hotel in Little Rock*

Michael Jordan

"That Michael Jackson is unbelievable, isn't he? He's just unbelievable."

—*Al Gore, at a Chicago Bulls game in January 1998*

Junkets

"This means we get to go to Europe!"

—*Marvella Bayh (wife of Indiana senator Birch Bayh), upon hearing that her husband had been elected to the U.S. Senate in 1962*

Juries

"I always wait until a jury has spoken before I anticipate what they will do."

—*Janet Reno (U.S. attorney general, 1993–)*

Legislation

"This legislation has far-reaching ramifistations."

—*Gib Lewis (Speaker, Texas House of Representatives, 1983–1993)*

Life

"Those who survived the San Francisco earthquake said, 'Thank God, I'm still alive.' But, of course, those who died—their lives will never be the same again."

> —*Barbara Boxer (senator from California, 1993–)*

"Livable"

"Last year, the vice president launched a new effort to help make communities more liberal."

> —*Bill Clinton, attempting to praise Al Gore in his January 2000 State of the Union address. He had meant to say "make communities more livable."*

Courtney Love

"I'm a really big fan."

> —*Al Gore, to rock star Courtney Love at a Hollywood party. Later, to* Spin *magazine, she said, "I was like, 'Yeah, right. Name a song, Al.'"*

Lust

"I've looked on many women with lust. I've commited adultery in my heart many times. God knows I will do this and forgives me."

> —*Jimmy Carter in an interview with* Playboy *one month before the 1976 presidential election*

"I was signing books and a very nice-looking young lady came by and said, 'Mr. President, if you're still lusting in your heart, I'm available.' The whole crowd broke out laughing. I blushed."

—*Jimmy Carter (president, 1977–1981)*

Lying

"Tell 'em I lied!"

—*Earl Long (governor of Louisiana, 1939–1940, 1949–1953, 1957–1960). After Long broke a campaign promise, a press aide asked Long how he should explain the situation to reporters.*

Male Pregnancy

"[To be in danger] you have to take PCBs in quantitites steadily over a period of time, and probably be pregnant, which I don't intend to be."

—*Hugh Carey (governor of New York, 1975–1982)*

Management

"I'm one of those mayors whose management style is to allow free and unlimited debate, to a point."

—*Marion Barry (former mayor of Washington, D.C.)*

Marijuana

"Only when committing adultery."

> —*Wyche Fowler (senator from Georgia, 1987–1992), when*
> *asked if he had smoked marijuana in the 1960s*

Marriage

"Well, I think that's a—it's had some difficult times, but I think we have—we, I think, have been able to make some very good progress and it's—I would say that it's—it's—it's delightful that we're able to—to share the time and the relationship that we—that we do share."

> —*Ted Kennedy (senator from Massachusetts, 1963–). In a*
> *November 4, 1979, interview, Roger Mudd of CBS asked,*
> *"What is the present state of your marriage?"*

Martians

"Wouldn't it be sad to have an Internet connection if there's no Martians to write to?"

> —*Bill Clinton, on futuristic technology*

Maturity

"Part of growing up is learning how to control one's impulses."

> —*Hillary Rodham Clinton, introducing President Clinton at*
> *an event promoting gun control*

McDonald's

"I don't necessarily consider McDonald's junk food."
> —*Bill Clinton*

Me

"I'm here! It's me! It's Mayor Koch! I'm here!"
> —*Ed Koch (mayor of New York, 1978–1989), hollering at East German guards near the Berlin Wall*

Monica

"You're not going to believe this—but—I want to tell you what's in the newspapers."
> —*Bill Clinton, to Hillary Rodham Clinton on January 21, 1998, when the Monica Lewinsky story broke in the* Washington Post. *Hillary said the story "came as a very big surprise."*

"I did not have sexual relations with that woman, Miss Lewinsky."
> —*Bill Clinton, on January 26, 1998, in the Roosevelt Room of the White House, while defiantly wagging his finger*

"If the dress doesn't fit, we must acquit. If it's on the dress, he must confess."
> —*James Traficant (representative from Ohio, 1985–)*

"The President looked me in the eye and told me the same thing on several occasions. And I'm not upset. You want to know why? Because I never believed him in the first place."

> —*Robert Torricelli (senator from New Jersey, 1997–), on Bill Clinton's denials of an affair with Monica Lewinsky*

"The stain on his presidency . . . is not going to be dry-cleaned out."

> —*Mike McCurry (press secretary to President Clinton, 1994–1998)*

"She's basically a good girl."

> —*Bill Clinton, on Monica Lewinsky*

Dick Morris

"I would kind of like to throw up in living color."

> —*Pat Schroeder (representative from Colorado, 1973–1996), on the revelation that Clinton strategist Dick Morris regularly paid $400 an hour for a prostitute, Sherry Rowland*

Mummies

"You know, if I were a single man, I might ask that mummy out. That's a good-looking nummy!"

> —*Bill Clinton, looking at "Juanita," a newly discovered Incan mummy*

NAFTA

"Mr. Speaker, the White House says NAFTA is creating new and exciting jobs. I did some research on those jobs: zipper trimmer, brassiere tender, jelly roller, bosom presser, chicken sexer, sanitary napkin specialist, and a panty-hose crotch closer machine operator. That is what I call exciting jobs, Mr. Speaker."

> —*James Traficant (representative from Ohio, 1985–)*

New Year's Resolutions

"I will try to keep the same hairdo for at least thirty days."

> —*Hillary Rodham Clinton, outlining her New Year's resolutions for 1996*

New York Yankees

"The fact is, I've always been a Yankees fan. As a young girl, I became very interested and enamored of the Yankees."

> —*Hillary Rodham Clinton, describing her childhood in Chicago*

Nuclear Power Plants

"Maine is a good location for a nuclear power plant—where the damn thing could have an accident and not hurt anybody."

> —*John Silber (candidate for governor of Massachusetts, 1990)*

Oakland

"There's nothing in Oakland I want."

> —Art Agnos (mayor of San Francisco, 1987–1991), declining
> to make a bet with Lionel Wilson, the mayor of Oakland,
> over the result of the 1989 World Series between the San
> Francisco Giants and the Oakland A's

O.J.

"I think you should talk to white people."

> —Maxine Waters (representative from California, 1991–),
> when asked if she was anxious to hear the verdict in the O.J.
> Simpson civil trial

Paintings

"It's probably a contradiction, like all things—men, women, night, day."

> —Hillary Rodham Clinton, waxing philosophical about a
> deep-blue painting inside an Egyptian temple

Passion

"I think it's just a reflection of her passion for the arts."

> —Gaston Caperton (governor of West Virginia, 1989–1996),
> after his wife, the conductor of the Wheeling Symphony,
> called Bob Dole an "idiot"

Percentages

"[I'm] a thousand percent for Eagleton . . . [and have] no intention of dropping him from the ticket."

> —*George McGovern, 1972 Democratic presidential nominee,*
> *on July 26, 1972, after it was revealed that his running mate,*
> *Senator Thomas Eagleton, had received shock therapy for*
> *depression. A few days later, McGovern forced Eagleton off*
> *the ticket.*

"The brave men who died in Vietnam, more than one hundred percent of which were black, were the ultimate sacrifice."

> —*Marion Barry (former mayor of Washington, D.C.)*

Perestroika

"This is just my contribution to perestroika."

> —*Charlie Wilson (representative from Texas, 1973–1996),*
> *when a reporter spotted him examining some lace panties in*
> *a Moscow lingerie store*

Playboy

"Think of it as coalition-building."

> —*Barney Frank (representative from Massachusetts, 1981–).*
> *Frank, who is gay, did an interview for* Playboy, *which*
> *appeared in an issue that also contained a photo spread*
> *on "The Girls of the Hawaiian Tropics."*

Police

"I promise you a police car on every sidewalk."

> —*Marion Barry (former mayor of Washington, D.C.)*

"The police are not here to create disorder. They're here to preserve disorder."

> —*Richard J. Daley (mayor of Chicago, 1955–1976)*

"Policemen should . . . shoot arsonists and looters: arsonists to kill and looters to maim and detain. You wouldn't want to shoot children, but with mace you could detain youngsters."

> —*Richard J. Daley (mayor of Chicago, 1955–1976). These were Daley's instructions to the police during the riots that followed the murder of Martin Luther King in 1968.*

"They are decent, family men."

> —*Richard J. Daley (mayor of Chicago, 1955–1976), responding to accusations of police stormtrooper tactics in Chicago*

"There's nothing wrong with this country that we couldn't cure by turning it over to the police for a couple of weeks."

> —*George Wallace (former governor of Alabama)*

Politics

"You always eat if somebody offers you food."

> —*Bill Clinton, telling his chauffeur during his 1974 congressional campaign that this was the "first rule of politics"*

"I seldom think of politics more than eighteen hours a day."

> —*Lyndon Johnson (president, 1963–1969)*

"If you can't drink their booze, take their money, fool with their women, and then vote against 'em, you don't belong in politics."

—*Jesse Unruh (California state representative, 1951–1969)*

Pollution

"I've always thought that underpopulated countries in Africa are vastly underpolluted."

>—*Lawrence Summers (Secretary of the Treasury, 1999–). Summers, then chief economist for the World Bank, was explaining why the United States should export toxic wastes to the Third World.*

Poor People

"I stay out of their way at Kmart."

>—*Willie Brown (mayor of San Francisco, 1996–), asked what he did to help the poor*

Popularity

"I am clearly more popular than Reagan. I am in my third term. Where's Reagan? Gone after two! Defeated by George Bush and Michael Dukakis, no less."

>—*Marion Barry (former Mayor of Washington, D.C.)*

Presidency

"Well, I'm—were I to make the announcement and to run—the reasons that I would run is because I have a great belief in this country, that it is—there's more natural resources than any nation of the world, there's the greatest educated population in the world, the greatest technology of any country in the world, and the greatest political system in the world."

> —*Ted Kennedy (senator from Massachusetts, 1963–). In a December 4, 1979, television interview, Roger Mudd of CBS asked Kennedy, "Why do you want to be president?"*

"Don't people understand? It's going to be more fun."

> —*Bill Clinton, asked how his presidency would be different*

Press Conferences

"We fully expect to be at least half as interesting as 'Home Improvement.'"

> —*Mike McCurry (press secretary to President Clinton, 1994–1998), after NBC and ABC refused to preempt sitcoms for a presidential press conference in 1995*

Private Enterprise

"The private enterprise system indicates that some people have higher incomes than others."

> —*Jerry Brown (governor of California, 1975–1982)*

Progress

"Sometimes in order to make progress and move ahead, you have to stand up and do the wrong thing."

—*Gary Ackerman (representative from New York, 1983–), rationalizing his vote for welfare reform*

Promiscuity

"I just have no firsthand experience."

—*Al Gore, when asked whether today's young women are too promiscuous*

Promises

"He kept the promises he meant to keep."

—*George Stephanopoulos (advisor to President Clinton, 1993–1996), referring to President Clinton*

Public Exposure

"Nixon has been sitting in the White House while George McGovern has been exposing himself to the people of the United States."

—*Frank Licht (governor of Rhode Island, 1969–1972), during the 1972 presidential campaign*

Pyramids

"I've always wanted to see the pyramids."

> —*Hamilton Jordan (chief of staff to President Carter, 1977–1981). Jordan, attending a Washington dinner party hosted by Barbara Walters, turned to the wife of the Egyptian ambassador and gazed at her "ample front."*

Q-tips

"Actually, we've been wondering why the office keeps receiving those huge boxes of Q-tips."

> —*Chris Lehabe (spokesman for Vice President Gore), after the vice president's office received a great deal of mail addressed to the CVS drugstore in Georgetown*

Queers

"I just can't figure out these queers. I hear they're all over Congress. Why would anyone want to be a queer?"

> —*Tip O'Neill (representative from Massachusetts, 1953–1986)*

"I've felt like the little Dutch boy with his finger in the dike."

> —*Pat Schroeder (representative from Colorado, 1973–1996), speaking to the Gertrude Stein Democratic Club of Washington, D.C., a gay and lesbian group. Schroeder was attempting to make a point about the damage done by the Reagan administration.*

Racism

"The laws in this city are clearly racist. All laws are racist. The law of gravity is racist."

—Marion Barry (former mayor of Washington, D.C.)

Radio Talk Shows

"I don't have time to talk to anyone who has time to call a radio program."

—Ann Richards (governor of Texas, 1991–1995), explaining why she had no interest in being a radio talk-show host

Reasoning

"That is unreasonable reasoning."

—Richard J. Daley (mayor of Chicago, 1955–1976), complaining to reporters

Recognition

"And now, will y'all stand up and be recognized."

—Gib Lewis (Speaker, Texas House of Representatives, 1982–1993), to a group of handicapped people in wheelchairs

Reincarnation

"I want to come back as me."

> —*Ed Koch (mayor of New York, 1978–1989)*

Relatives

"Rodman. Rodham. Are we related?"

> —*Hillary Rodham Clinton, to Dennis Rodman, after he gave her a basketball jersey in Chicago*

Religion

"He goes down by the Potomac and listens to hymns, as the cleansing water of the Potomac goes by, and we're going to wash all the Sodomites and fornicators out of town."

> —*James Carville (Democratic political consultant), mocking the religious faith of Kenneth Starr*

Republican Budget

"By comparison, it makes *Rosemary's Baby* look like a dream child."

> —*J. James Exon (senator from Nebraska, 1979–1996), on Republican budget proposals*

Republican Party

"I always liked small parties, and the Republican Party is just about the size I like."

> —*Lyndon Johnson (president, 1963–1969)*

"You should be here with us today. There's no snow and no Republicans."

> —*Willie Brown (mayor of San Francisco, 1996–), on the phone with President Clinton. Brown was describing his inauguration as mayor, while Washington, D.C., was experiencing a blizzard.*

"Republican Party, I wish you well. May you never be hated by Tonya Harding and never be loved by Lorena Bobbitt."

> —*James Traficant (representative from Ohio, 1985–)*

"A black man voting for the Republicans makes as much sense as a chicken voting for Colonel Sanders."

> —*J. C. Watts, Sr. (father of J. C. Watts, Jr., an Oklahoma Republican congressman)*

Resentment

"I resent your insinuendos."

> —*Richard J. Daley (mayor of Chicago, 1955–1976)*

Responsibilities

"I am not the leader of Washington. I am not the business leader of Washington. I am not the spiritual leader of Washington. I am not the civic leader of Washington. I am not the social leader of Washington. I am the political leader of Washington. That's where my responsibility ends."

—*Marion Barry (former mayor of Washington, D.C.)*

Scandal

"All I was asked about by the press is a woman I didn't sleep with and a draft I didn't dodge."

—*Bill Clinton, on* Nightline *in 1992*

"I have nothing else to say. We—we did—if—the—the—I—I—the stories are just as they have been said."

—*Bill Clinton*

"I have acknowledged wrongdoing. I have acknowledged causing pain in my marriage. I have said things to you and to the American people from the beginning that no American politician ever has. I think most Americans watching this tonight will know what we're saying. They'll get it and they'll know that we have been more candid, and I think what the press has to decide is, are we going to engage in a game of 'gotcha'?"

—*Bill Clinton, on* 60 Minutes *after the 1992 Super Bowl*

Security Detail

"People have criticized me because my security detail is larger than the President's. But you must ask yourself: Are there more people who want to kill me than who want to kill the President? I can assure you there are."

—*Marion Barry (former mayor of Washington, D.C.)*

Segregation

"Segregation now, segregation tomorrow, segregation forever."

—*George Wallace (former governor of Alabama), in his 1963 inaugural address*

Self-Perception

"I came here as prime steak and now I feel like low-grade hamburger."

—*Joycelyn Elders (surgeon general, 1993–1994), comparing life in Little Rock to life in Washington, D.C.*

"I'm old. I'm young. I'm intelligent. I'm stupid."

—*Warren Beatty (Democratic Party activist)*

Sex

"My theory is, don't do it before you're twenty-one and then don't tell me about it."

—*Hillary Rodham Clinton*

"The Gulf War was like teenage sex. We got in too soon and out too soon."

> —*Tom Harkin (senator from Iowa, 1985–)*

"Hattie, I'm horny."

> —*Bruce Babbitt (governor of Arizona, 1979–1987), to his wife during the 1988 Democratic presidential campaign*

"I was never worried about any sex investigation in Washington. All the men on my staff can type."

> —*Bella Abzug (representative from New York, 1971–1977)*

"Have you stopped wearing your wife's lingerie? Have you stopped messing around with little boys?"

> —*Gus Savage (representative from Illinois, 1981–1992), answering reporters' questions about his sexual activities*

"That's garbage. Why can't they catch me in a sex scandal? I could use some good publicity."

> —*Willie Brown (mayor of San Francisco, 1996–), on an FBI investigation into his financial ties to a garbage company*

"This attractive lady whom I had only recently been introduced to dropped into my lap. . . . I chose not to dump her off."

> —*Gary Hart (senator from Colorado, 1975–1986), referring to an encounter with Donna Rice*

"If I don't have a woman every three days or so I get a terrible headache."

> —*John Kennedy*

"We need laws that protect everyone. Men and women, straights and gays, regardless of sexual perversion . . . ah, persuasion."

> —*Bella Abzug (representative from New York, 1971–1977),*
> *speaking at a rally for the Equal Rights Amendment*

"I appreciate Representative Frank trying to enhance my dull image, but in terms of obsession with sex, I'm not in Barney's league."

> —*Sam Nunn (senator from Georgia, 1972–1996), in response*
> *to Congressman Barney Frank's statement that Nunn was*
> *"obsessed with sex and involved in an anti-gay witch hunt"*

"The only woman I have had conjugal relations with is my wife."

> —*Chuck Robb (senator from Virginia, 1989–), defending him-*
> *self after revelations that he received a nude massage in a*
> *hotel room from Tai Collins, a former Playmate*

Shoes

"I feel like I spent the last year in Imelda Marcos's closet."

> —*Paul Begala (former Clinton White House political advisor),*
> *asked whether he would return to the White House "if*
> *another shoe drops"*

Showers

"It shows as an elected official I'm squeaky clean, with nothing to hide."

> —*Frank Jordan (mayor of San Francisco, 1992–1995), explaining why he posed nude in a shower with two local disc jockeys during his 1995 reelection campaign*

Simplicity

"I want only two houses, rather than seven. . . . I feel like letting go of things."

> —*Barbra Streisand (Democratic political activist)*

Skeletons

"[I have] more skeletons in my closet than the Smithsonian."

> —*Ben Jones (representative from Georgia, 1989–1992), a former alcoholic once charged with battering his ex-wife*

Sleep

"I wish I didn't have to sleep at all for a year."

> —*Bill Clinton, expressing regret that he had only one more year in office*

Small Businessman

"I've been out here struggling as a small businessman."
>—*Bill Bradley (2000 presidential candidate), in May 1999. Bradley earned more than $2 million in 1998 making speeches.*

Smoking

"I don't believe all that stuff about smoking hurting you."
>—*Billy Carter (brother of President Jimmy Carter)*

Soda

"Who knew cream soda had caffeine in it?"
>—*Bill Bradley, analyzing the cause of his irregular heartbeats*

Soup Kitchens

"Do you come here often?"
>—*Ted Kennedy (senator from Massachusetts, 1963–), to a woman at a Brooklyn soup kitchen*

Speechifying

"And now, in conclusion . . ."
>—*Bill Clinton, at the end of his thirty-two-minute speech at the 1988 Democratic National Convention. The crowd erupted in applause.*

"I never thought my speeches were too long. I enjoyed them."

> —*Hubert Humphrey (vice president, 1965–1969)*

"Ladies and gentlemen, it is a great pleasure to be with you today. For immediate release only."

> —*Joseph Montoya (senator from New Mexico, 1964–1976), reading a prepared text at a political dinner*

Joseph Stalin

"I like Stalin. He is straightforward."

> —*Harry Truman (president, 1945–1953), assessing the Soviet dictator after their first meeting*

"I believe we are going to get along very well with him and the Russian people—very well indeed."

> —*Franklin Delano Roosevelt, in a 1963 Fireside Chat*

Kenneth Starr

"Ken Starr is one mistake away from not having any kneecaps."

> —*James Carville (Democratic political consultant)*

"As with mosquitoes, horseflies, and most bloodsucking parasites, Kenneth Starr was spawned in stagnant water."

> —*James Carville*

Stewardesses

"Stockpile Stewardesses Program."

> —*Ted Kennedy (senator from Massachusetts, 1963–). He apparently meant to show his support for the "Stockpile Stewardship Program," which was part of a nuclear test ban treaty.*

Strip Joints

"First, it was not a strip bar; it was an erotic club. And second, what can I say? I'm a night owl."

> —*Marion Barry (former mayor of Washington, D.C.), responding to reports on his late-night activities*

Suburban Life

"Have you ever lived in the suburbs? It's sterile. It's wasting your life."

> —*Ed Koch (mayor of New York, 1978–1989), in a* Playboy *interview in 1982, while running for governor of New York*

Suitcases

"Hey, if Barney Frank can come out of the closet, I can come out of the suitcase."

> —*Tip O'Neill (representative from Massachusetts, 1953–1986), on public opposition to his numerous commercial endorsements, including one where he popped out of a suitcase*

Tobacco

"I've plowed the ground, put in the seed beds, I've planted it, hoed it, wormed it, suckered it, cut it, spiked it, put it in the barns, stripped it, and sold it. I know what it's about, how important that way of life is."

> —*Al Gore*

Trailer Park Trash

"Drag a hundred-dollar bill through a trailer park, you never know what you'll find."

> —*James Carville (Democratic political consultant), in response to Paula Jones's accusation of sexual harassment by Bill Clinton*

Truth

"Eight more days and I can start telling you the truth again. It's killing me, I'll tell you."

> —*Christopher Dodd (senator from Connecticut, 1981–), on the Don Imus radio show just before the 1996 presidential election*

Turkeys

"There are so many turkeys in Washington, I should pardon at least one."

> —*Bill Clinton, explaining why he spared the ceremonial White House turkey the day before Thanksgiving in 1995*

Two Words

"I hope that history will present me with maybe two words. One is peace. The other is human rights."

> —*Jimmy Carter (president, 1977–1981)*

Underwear

"Usually briefs."

> —*Bill Clinton, during an MTV "Choose or Lose" election special in 1992. A young woman asked, "The world is dying to know: Is it boxers or briefs?" Clinton laughed, saying, "I can't believe she asked that."*

Vagueness

"A little vagueness goes a long way in this business."

> —*Jerry Brown (governor of California, 1975–1982)*

Vast Right-Wing Conspiracy

"[He is getting support from] the extreme right wing, the extra chromosome right wing."

> —*Al Gore, describing supporters of Oliver North's 1994 Senate candidacy. An extra chromosome results in Down's syndrome. Gore made this remark during Down's Syndrome Awareness Month.*

Velcro

"You don't want to look like you're trying to Velcro yourself to the President."

> —*Mack McLarty (former chief of staff to President Clinton), explaining why he was taking an office in the basement of the White House rather than the West Wing*

Vice Presidency

"The vice presidency of the United States isn't worth a pitcher of warm spit."

> —*John Nance Gardner (vice president, 1933–1941)*

"All that Hubert needs over there is a gal to answer the phone and a pencil with an eraser on it."

> —*Lyndon Johnson (president, 1977–1981), referring to Hubert Humphrey, his vice president*

"'Your Adequacy' is okay."

> —*Al Gore, asked by David Letterman what he would like to be called*

Vietnam

"You pissed on my rug."

> —*Lyndon Johnson (president, 1963–1969), to journalist Lester Pearson, after Pearson called for a temporary halt to the bombing of North Vietnam*

"Wasn't Dean Rusk a really good secretary of state, apart from Vietnam?"

> —*Jody Powell (press secretary to President Carter)*

"No sane person in the country likes the war in Vietnam, and neither does President Johnson."

> —*Hubert Humphrey (vice president, 1965–1969)*

"If you have a mother-in-law with only one eye and she has it in the center of her forehead, you don't keep her in the living room."

> —*Lyndon Johnson (president, 1963–1969), on his unwillingness to discuss American military progress in Vietnam*

Vocabulary

"The use of a two-syllable vulgarity by the chairman was rather ambitious."

> —Mike McCurry (press secretary to President Clinton, 1994–1998), commenting on Indiana Republican congressman Dan Burton, who called President Clinton "a scumbag"

Voting

"The voters are going to decide who is elected and who is not."

> —Al Gore, explaining the electoral process on Larry King Live

"He didn't get enough votes."

> —Richard J. Daley (mayor of Chicago, 1955–1976), explaining why Hubert Humphrey, the 1968 Democratic presidential nominee, didn't carry Illinois

"Students don't vote. Do you expect me to come in here and kiss your ass?"

> —Wyche Fowler (senator from Georgia, 1977–1982), speaking to a group of volunteers campaigning for a balanced federal budget

Water Mains

"People blame me because these water mains break, but I ask you: If the water mains didn't break, would it be my responsibility to fix them? Would it?"

> —Marion Barry (former mayor of Washington, D.C.)

Water Pollution

"[They] drink and bathe in Perrier."

> —*Pete Stark (representative from California, 1973–), explaining why Republicans are willing to reduce the budget for clean water*

White Folks

"White folks was in caves while we was building empires. . . . We taught philosophy and astrology and mathematics before Socrates and them Greek homos ever got around to it."

> —*Al Sharpton (New York City Democratic political activist), in a 1994 speech at Kean College in New Jersey*

White House

"I don't know whether it's the finest public housing in America or the crown jewel of the federal prison system."

> —*Bill Clinton*

Whitewater

"Here's a quarter. Call someone who cares."

> —*James Carville (Democratic political consultant), asked about the Whitewater convictions of Jim McDougal, Susan McDougal, and Jim Guy Tucker*

Winter

"If elected, there will never be another winter in Iowa! Let the word go forth!"

> —Bill Bradley (2000 Democratic presidential candidate), while campaigning in Iowa

Women

"Bitch set me up."

> —Marion Barry (former mayor of Washington, D.C.), complaining about a former girlfriend, Rasheeda Moore, who cooperated with an FBI sting operation that resulted in Barry's arrest for cocaine possession

"All my life I've been looking for a woman as tall as I am."

> —Bill Clinton, at a White House ceremony honoring the University of North Carolina women's basketball team for winning the 1994 NCAA championship. He put his arm around Gwendolyn Gillingham, the team's 6'7" center.

"Sensible and responsible women do not want to vote."

> —Grover Cleveland (president, 1885–1889, 1893–1897)

"I am not a chauvinist, obviously. . . . I believe in women's rights for every woman but my own."

> —Harold Washington (mayor of Chicago, 1984–1987)

"I cook occasionally just to see how easy women's work is."

> —Tip O'Neill (representative from Massachusetts, 1953–1986)

"Politics gives guys so much power that they tend to behave badly around women. And I hope I never get into that."

> —*Bill Clinton, to a woman friend while he was a Rhodes scholar at Oxford*

"Women prefer Democrats to men."

> —*Tony Coelho (representative from California, 1979–1989)*

"I don't believe I could have chosen a woman to be vice president who cares more about day-care centers, care for the deprived, and women's rights than Fritz Mondale."

> —*Jimmy Carter (president, 1977–1981)*

Work

"Hard work is damn near as overrated as monogamy."

> —*Huey Long (governor of Louisiana, 1928–1932)*

The World

"I see the world in very fluid, contradictory, emerging, interconnected terms, and with that kind of circuitry I just don't feel the need to say what is going to happen or will not happen."

> —*Jerry Brown (governor of California, 1975–1982)*

THE

267

STUPIDEST

THINGS

Republicans

EVER SAID

BY

TED RUETER

THREE RIVERS PRESS
NEW YORK

Published by Three Rivers Press, New York, New York. Member of the Crown Publishing Group.

Random House, Inc. New York, Toronto, London, Sydney, Auckland
www.randomhouse.com

THREE RIVERS PRESS is a registered trademark and the Three Rivers Press colophon is a trademark of Random House, Inc.

Printed in the United States of America

Designed by Susan Maksuta

Library of Congress Cataloging-in-Publication Data
Rueter, Ted.
The 267 stupidest things Republicans have ever said—the 267 stupidest things Democrats have ever said / by Ted Rueter—1st ed.
    p. cm.
1. United States—Politics and government—1945–1989—Humor. 2. United States—Politics and government—1989—Humor. 3. United States—Politics and government—1945–1989—Quotations, maxims, etc. 4. United States—Politics and government—1989—Quotations, maxims, etc. 5. Politicians—United States—Quotations. 6. Politicians—United States—Humor. 7. Republican Party (U.S. : 1854–)—Humor. 8. Democratic Party (U.S.)—Humor. 9. American wit and humor. I. Title.
E838.3 .R84 2000
973.92'02'07—dc21
                                 99-59995

ISBN 0-609-80635-1

10 9 8 7

First Edition

Actors

"What does an actor know about politics?"

> —*Ronald Reagan, criticizing Ed Asner (then president of the Screen Actors Guild) for opposing American foreign policy*

Accountability

"Does a bank president know when a bank teller is fiddling around with the books? No."

> —*Donald T. Regan (White House Chief of Staff under Ronald Reagan), explaining how $30 million could have been paid to the Nicaraguan Contras without the administration's knowledge.*

African-Americans

"I'll hire blacks as long as they can do the cotton-pickin' job."

> —*Evan Mecham (governor of Arizona, 1987–1988)*

"I have a lot of African-American friends."

> —*Larry Pressler (senator from South Dakota, 1979–1996), explaining how he was going to be elected mayor of Washington, D.C. He eventually decided not to run.*

Lamar Alexander

"Let me tell you, you can get a lot of those Howdy Doody shirts for cheap today."

> —*Pat Buchanan (1996 Republican presidential candidate),*
> *referring to Lamar Alexander's trademark red-and-black-*
> *checkered shirts, on the day that Alexander dropped out of*
> *the 1996 presidential race*

Ambassadorships

"I understand it's a nice lifestyle. I love golf, and I understand they have a lot of nice golf courses."

> —*Chic Hecht (senator from Nevada, 1983–1988), explaining*
> *why he wanted to be ambassador to the Bahamas. Shortly*
> *after this statement, he got the job!*

"This is a man who was not only the president of the National Council of Shopping Centers, but the *International* Council of Shopping Centers in 1986, and traveled around the world."

> —*Rudy Boschwitz (senator from Minnesota, 1978–1991), in a*
> *letter asking the Reagan administration to name Melvin F.*
> *Sembler ambassador to Australia. Sembler got the job.*

Americans

"Wherever I have gone in this country, I have found Americans."
> —*Alf Landon (1936 Republican presidential nominee)*

"The American people is very supportive of me."

> —*George W. Bush (governor of Texas, 1995–), during an interview with Jane Clayson of CBS.*

Antichrist

"Who will the Antichrist be? I don't know. Nobody else knows. Of course, he'll be Jewish."

> —*Jerry Falwell (president, Moral Majority, 1979–1990)*

Anti-Semitism

"I hope I stand for anti-bigotry, anti-Semitism, anti-racism."

> —*George Bush*

Apologies

"I will never apologize for the United States of America—I don't care what the facts are."

> —*George Bush, speaking to Republican ethnic leaders in 1988 after the unintentional downing of an Iranian airplane. Bush also said, "I'm not an apologize-for-America kind of guy."*

"I'm apologizing for the conduct that it was alleged that I did."

> —*Robert Packwood (senator from Oregon, 1969–1995). Packwood was accused of sexually harassing dozens of women. He claimed that he didn't remember anything.*

Argentina

"You cannot be president of the United States if you don't have faith. Remember Lincoln, going to his knees in times of trial and the Civil War and all that stuff. You can't be. And we are blessed. So don't feel sorry for—don't cry for me, Argentina. Message: I care."

—George Bush, to employees of an insurance company during the 1992 New Hampshire presidential primary

Arithmetic

"Mr. Nixon was the thirty-seventh President of the United States. He had been preceded by thirty-six others."

—Gerald Ford (president, 1974–1977)

Astrology

"I've not tied my life by it, but I won't answer the question the other way because I don't know enough about it to say, is there something to it or not."

—Ronald Reagan, asked if he believed in astrology—after it was revealed that his wife Nancy regularly consulted an astrologer for advice on the President's schedule

Auschwitz

"Boy, they were big on crematoriums, weren't they?"

—George Bush, touring Auschwitz in 1987

Bedfellows

"I've got to be careful about who I get in bed with."

> —*George Bush, commenting on Democratic Party support he received for leaving the National Rifle Association*

Bob

"We've never had a president named Bob, and I think it's time."

> —*Bob Dole (1996 Republican presidential nominee), announcing his presidential candidacy in 1995*

Bondage

"Republicans understand the importance of bondage between a mother and child."

> —*Dan Quayle*

Brainwashing

"I just had the greatest brainwashing that anybody can get when you go over to Vietnam . . . not only by the generals, but also by the diplomatic corps over there."

> —*George Romney (governor of Michigan, 1963–1969). Romney had been the front-runner for the 1968 Republican presidential nomination. This statement effectively ended his campaign. Minnesota senator Eugene McCarthy, a 1968 Democratic presidential candidate, cracked that a brainwashing wasn't necessary, since "a light rinse would have been sufficient."*

Budget Deficit

"I am not worried about the deficit. It is big enough to take care of itself."

—Ronald Reagan

George Bush

"We have been pushing the idea that George Bush is going to make things much, much worse."

—Dan Quayle

Campaign Contributions

"Some of us are uncomfortable taking honoraria. I am uncomfortable taking campaign contributions. So I compromised; I decided to take both."

—Bob Dole (1996 Republican presidential nominee)

Caribou

"If you're worried about caribou, take a look at the arguments that were used about the pipeline. They'd say the caribou would be extinct. You've got to shake them away with a stick. They're all making love lying up against the pipeline, and you got thousands of caribou up there."

—George Bush, commenting on the Alaskan pipeline

Century

"[The Holocaust] was an obscene period in our nation's history . . . this century's history. . . . We all lived in this century. I didn't live in this century."

—*Dan Quayle*

Chastity

"I'm not talking about scratching where it tickles; I'm talking about screwing."

—*Jeremiah Denton (senator from Alabama, 1981–1986). After proposing funding for teenage chastity centers, Senator Denton was asked what he meant by juvenile promiscuity.*

Child Labor

"What's wrong with saying that when school's out, you can hire kids as young as twelve or thirteen?"

—*Newt Gingrich (Speaker, U.S. House of Representatives, 1995–1998)*

Childhood Memories

"We always went there eagerly awaiting the arrival of the next edition of *National Geographic* to look at all those ladies from faraway places who were topless in the magazine."

—*Phil Gramm (senator from Texas, 1985–), discussing his use of the local library as a kid*

Clarity

"[The question] is too suppository."

—Alexander Haig (Secretary of State, 1981–1982), responding to a question at a Senate hearing

Bill Clinton

"Bill Clinton's foreign policy experience is pretty much limited to having had breakfast once at the International House of Pancakes."

—Pat Buchanan (1996 Republican presidential candidate)

"Mr. Clinton better watch out if he comes down here. He'd better have a bodyguard."

—Jesse Helms (senator from North Carolina, 1973–)

"We've never said to the press that Clinton is a philandering, pot-smoking draft dodger."

—Mary Matalin (1992 Bush deputy campaign manager)

"My dog Millie knows more about foreign policy than those two bozos."

—George Bush, on Bill Clinton and Al Gore

Hillary Rodham Clinton

"Hillary believes that twelve-year-olds should have a right to sue their parents, and she has compared marriage as an institution to slavery."

—Pat Buchanan (1996 Republican presidential candidate)

"Hillary Clinton in an apron is like Michael Dukakis in a tank."

> —*Roger Ailes (Republican political consultant)*

Compassion

"I'm the Compassionate Hammer."

> —*Tom DeLay (representative from Texas, 1985–), known as*
> *"The Hammer" for his hard-nosed tactics*

Congress

"There are lots more people in the House. I don't know exactly—
I've never counted, but at least a couple hundred."

> —*Dan Quayle, explaining the difference between the House*
> *and the Senate*

Constitution

"You don't have many suspects who are innocent of a crime.
That's contradictory. If a person is innocent of a crime, then he is
not a suspect."

> —*Ed Meese (United States attorney general, 1985–1988)*

"It's perfectly legal. I drive my American-made car to work as
provided for in the Constitution."

> —*Roger Jepsen (senator from Iowa, 1979–1985). In April 1993,*
> *Senator Jepsen was stopped by a northern Virginia police-*
> *woman for driving alone in a car-pool lane. He refused to*
> *pay the $35 ticket, claiming congressional immunity.*

Cookies

"I was dramatically shaped by my grandmother and my aunts because they convinced me there was always a cookie available. Deep down inside me, I'm four years old, and I wake up and think out there, there's a cookie. Every morning I'm going, you know, either it can be baked or it's already been bought, but it's in a jar . . . somewhere. . . . And so that means when you open up the cupboard and the cookie isn't there, I don't say, 'Gee, there's no cookie.' I say, 'I wonder where it is.'"

> —*Newt Gingrich (Speaker, U.S. House of Representatives, 1995–1998), in his 1994 "Renewing American Civilization" lectures*

Courtship

"As a single member of the faculty, I am very interested in you coming to Texas A and M."

> —*Phil Gramm (senator from Texas, 1985–). Gramm was speaking to Wendy Lee, an applicant for a professorship at Texas A & M. Her response: "Yuck." They got married six weeks after she arrived on campus.*

Crime

"I am not a crook."
> —*Richard Nixon*

"The streets are safe in Philadelphia. It's only the people who make them unsafe."

> —*Frank Rizzo (mayor of Philadelphia, 1972–1980)*

"When the President does it, that means it's not illegal."
> —*Richard Nixon*

Charles de Gaulle

"This is a great day for France!"
> —*Richard Nixon, attending French president Charles de Gaulle's funeral*

Democracy

"Democracy used to be a good thing, but now it has gotten into the wrong hands."
> —*Jesse Helms (senator from North Carolina, 1973–)*

Democrats

"Democrats are the party of total bizarreness, total weirdness."
> —*Newt Gingrich (Speaker, U.S. House of Representatives, 1995–1998)*

"Coke-snorting, wife-swapping, baby-born-out-of-wedlock radical Hollywood leftists."
> —*Bob Dornan (representative from California, 1977–1983, 1985–1996), describing supporters of California Democratic senator Barbara Boxer*

"That giant masquerade ball up at Madison Square Garden—where twenty thousand radicals and liberals came dressed as moderates and centrists in the greatest single exhibition of cross-dressing in American political history."

—Pat Buchanan (1996 Republican presidential candidate), on the 1992 Democratic National Convention

Diversity

"We have every mixture you can have. I have a black, I have a woman, two Jews, and a cripple."

—James Watt (Secretary of the Interior, 1981–1983), describing an Interior Department advisory group

The Dodgers

"The Brooklyn Dodgers had a no-hitter last night . . ."

—Bob Dole, during his 1996 campaign. The Dodgers moved to Los Angeles in 1958.

Dogs

"It has been said by some cynic, maybe it was a former president, 'If you want a friend in Washington, get a dog.' We took them literally—that advice—as you know. But I didn't need that, because I have Barbara Bush."

—George Bush

Drought

"Pray for rain."

> —*Marlin Fitzwater (press secretary to Presidents Reagan and Bush), asked in 1988 about the Reagan administration's policies for responding to a drought*

Drugs

"I didn't intend for this to take on a political tone. I'm just here for the drugs."

> —*Nancy Reagan, asked a political question during a "Just Say No" rally*

"No to cocaine. No to marijuana. And a question mark over Jack Daniel's."

> —*Pat Buchanan (1996 Republican presidential candidate)*

Earthquakes

"Well, it looks as if the top part fell on the bottom part."

> —*Dan Quayle, commenting on the collapsed section of the 880 freeway after the San Francisco earthquake of 1989*

East Coast

"This country would be better off if we saw off the Eastern seaboard and let it float out to sea."

> —*Barry Goldwater (1964 Republican presidential nominee)*

Education

"We don't need some character in the Department of Education with sandals and beads telling us how to educate our children."

> —*Pat Buchanan (1996 Republican presidential candidate)*

Elderly

"The elderly eat less."

> —*S. I. Hayakawa (senator from California, 1977–1982), explaining why the elderly don't need special food-stamp eligibility*

Elections

"My supporters were at their daughters' coming-out parties or teeing up at the golf course for that crucial last round."

> —*George Bush, explaining why he didn't win the 1987 Iowa Republican presidential straw poll*

Endangered Species

"A species goes out of existence every twenty seconds. Surely a new species must come into existence every twenty seconds."

> —*Helen Chenoweth (representative from Idaho, 1995–)*

"We don't have to worry about endangered species. Why, we can't even get rid of the cockroach."

> —*James Watt (Secretary of the Interior, 1981–1983)*

Environment

"America's lands may be ravaged as a result of the actions of the environmentalists."

> *—James Watt (Secretary of the Interior, 1981–1983)*

"Excuse me, but can someone please explain what an ecosystem is?"

> *—Helen Chenoweth (representative from Idaho, 1995–)*

"Nutty left-wing goo-goo stuff."

> *—Newt Gingrich (Speaker, U.S. House of Representatives, 1995–1998), offering his analysis of Al Gore's book,* Earth in the Balance

Executions

"The President ought to be allowed to hang two men every year without giving any reason or explanation."

> *—Herbert Hoover (president, 1929–1933)*

Facts

"Facts are stupid things."

> *—Ronald Reagan, at the 1988 Republican National Convention. He meant to quote John Adams, who said, "Facts are stubborn things."*

Family Values

"Saint . . . Saint . . . ask my wife."

> —*Michael Huffington (representative from California, 1992–1993), asked what school his children attended*

"My family worked for everything we had. We even had a deed from the King of England for property in South Carolina. Now these jerks come along and try to give it to the Communists."

> —*Martha Mitchell (wife of John Mitchell, attorney general in the Nixon administration)*

"I think we need to keep good people in the race. So I've thought about ways to help McCain."

> —*Bob Dole (1996 Republican presidential nominee), referring to 2000 presidential candidate John McCain—in spite of the fact that his own wife, Elizabeth, was in the race*

"My name is Ronald Reagan. What's yours?"

> —*Ronald Reagan, introducing himself after giving the commencement address for a prep school in Scottsdale, Arizona, in 1964. The other person responded, "I'm your son Mike." Reagan said, "Oh. I didn't recognize you."*

Feminists

"The feminist agenda . . . is not about equal rights for women. It is about a socialist, anti-family political movement that encourages women to leave their husbands, kill their children, practice witchcraft, and become lesbians."

> —*Pat Robertson (1988 Republican presidential candidate)*

Food

"What am I supposed to order?"

> —*Ronald Reagan, to an aide while standing in line at*
> *McDonald's in Tuscaloosa, Alabama*

Steve Forbes

"If you can't make an issue of a guy who's got a 151-foot yacht,
you ought to hang it up."

> —*Pat Buchanan (1996 Republican presidential candidate)*

Fraternities

"Where fraternities are not allowed, Communism flourishes. The
fraternity system is a bastion of American strength."

> —*Barry Goldwater (1964 Republican presidential nominee).*
> *Goldwater called Harvard University a "Communist cell"*
> *because it had no fraternities in 1960.*

Freedom

"A mere forty years ago, beach volleyball was just beginning. No
bureaucrat would have invented it, and that's what freedom is all
about."

> —*Newt Gingrich (Speaker, U.S. House of Representatives,*
> *1995–1998)*

"There ought to be limits to freedom."

> —*George W. Bush, governor of Texas, after unsuccessfully filing a lawsuit to shut down a political parody site,*
> www.georgew.bush.com

Future

"We see nothing but increasingly brighter clouds every month."

> —*Gerald Ford (president, 1974–1977), speaking to a group of Michigan businessmen about the economy*

Gays

"I don't hate homosexuals. I don't even know any homosexuals."

> —*Jesse Helms (senator from North Carolina, 1973–)*

"The gentleman from Wisconsin didn't tell you when he was debating this amendment that he has a revolving door on his closet. He's in, he's out, he's in."

> —*Bob Dornan (representative from California, 1977–1983, 1985–1996), commenting on Steve Gunderson, a gay Republican congressman from Wisconsin*

"You should still love that person. You should not try to mistreat them as outcasts. Others have a sex addiction or are kleptomaniacs."

> —*Trent Lott (senator from Mississippi, 1989–)*

"Barney Fag."

>*—Dick Armey (representative from Texas, 1985–), referring to Massachusetts Democratic congressman Barney Frank. Armey claimed that it was an "inadvertent mispronunciation." Frank responded that this was unlikely, since no one had ever called his mother "Elsie Fag" during her fifty-nine years of marriage.*

Gender

"If you talk about being in combat, what does combat mean? If combat means being in a ditch, females have biological problems being in a ditch for thirty days because they get infections, and they don't have upper-body strength. I mean, some do, but they're relatively rare. On the other hand, men are basically little piglets. You drop them in the ditch, they roll around in it, doesn't matter, you know. These things are very real. On the other hand, if combat means being in an Aegis-class cruiser managing the computer controls for twelve ships and their rockets, a female again may be dramatically better than a male, who gets very, very frustrated sitting in a chair all the time because males are biologically driven to go out and hunt giraffes."

>*—Newt Gingrich (Speaker, U.S. House of Representatives, 1995–1998)*

"Atta, uh, girl . . . person . . . what are you, anyway?"

>*—Jesse Helms (senator from North Carolina, 1973–) to Senator Paula Hawkins. He was attempting to praise her.*

Geography

"I love California. I practically grew up in Phoenix."
> —*Dan Quayle*

Gift Receiving

"I didn't accept it. I received it."
> —*Richard Allen (National Security Advisor to President Reagan), justifying the two watches and $1,000 in cash he accepted from two Japanese journalists for helping to arrange an interview with Nancy Reagan*

Al Gore

"A bona fide tree-hugging, spotted-owl-loving, snail-darter-protecting, Gaia-worshiping, radical doomsday prophet."
> —*Rush Limbaugh (radio talk-show host)*

"Ozone Man, Ozone. He's crazy, way out, far out, man."
> —*George Bush, during the 1992 presidential campaign*

Governors

"I don't know. I've never played a governor."
> —*Ronald Reagan, asked by a reporter in 1966, "What kind of governor would you be?"*

Great Wall

"This is, indeed, a great wall."

> —*Richard Nixon, viewing the Great Wall of China*

Gridlock

"Our intent will not be to create gridlock. Oh, except maybe from time to time."

> —*Bob Dole (1996 Republican presidential nominee), on prospects for bipartisan cooperation with the Clinton administration*

Guns

"I own more shotguns than I need. But less shotguns than I want."

> —*Phil Gramm (senator from Texas, 1985–)*

"If guns are outlawed, how can we shoot the liberals?"

> —*Mike Gunn (Mississippi state senator, 1991–)*

Hawaii

"Hawaii is a unique state. It is a small state. It is a state that is by itself. It is a—it is different than the other states. Well, *all* states are different, but it's got a particularly unique situation."

> —*Dan Quayle, rebutting Bill Clinton's assertion that Hawaii's universal health care system was a model for the nation*

Hearts

"I keep it in a quart jar on my desk."

—*Phil Gramm (senator from Texas, 1985–), assuring an audience that he did indeed have a heart*

High School

"We're subsidizing dating. We're maintaining a fabric of education within which they can pursue their social life."

—*Newt Gingrich (Speaker, U.S. House of Representatives, 1995–1998), suggesting that students be encouraged to finish high school in less than four years*

Hippies

"If you tell me hippies and yippies are going to be able to do the job of helping America, I'll tell you this: they can't run a bus; they can't serve in a government office; they can't run a lathe in a factory. All they can do is lay down in the park and sleep or kick policemen."

—*Spiro Agnew (vice president, 1969–1973)*

History

"Well, I just think that from my strictly historical view of the twentieth century, that it probably, that is, you know, the best book I've certainly read. And he goes through it; he starts around the turn of the century up through Vietnam. And it is a very good historical book about history."

—*Dan Quayle, bragging that he had read Paul Johnson's book* Modern Times *during an August vacation*

Hitler

"Though Hitler was was indeed racist and anti-Semitic to the core, a man who without compunction could commit murder and genocide, he was also an individual of great courage, a soldier's soldier in the Great War, a political organizer of the first rank, a leader steeped in the history of Europe, who possessed oratorical powers that could awe even those who despised him."

—*Pat Buchanan (1996 Republican presidential candidate)*

Homelessness

"What we have found in this country, and maybe we're more aware of it now, is one problem that we've had, even in the best of times, and that is the people who are sleeping on the grates, the homeless who are homeless, you might say, by choice."

—*Ronald Reagan*

Hubert Humphrey

"Hubert Humphrey talks so fast that listening to him is like trying to read *Playboy* magazine with your wife turning the pages."

—Barry Goldwater (1964 Republican presidential nominee)

Saddam Hussein

"A go-getter."

—George Hansen (senator from Idaho, 1975–1984)

"When I need a little free advice about Saddam Hussein, I turn to country music."

—George Bush, at a country music awards ceremony in Nashville

Hypotheticals

"If a frog had wings, he wouldn't hit his tail on the ground. Too hypothetical."

—George Bush, during a 1992 campaign trip to New Hampshire, on extending unemployment benefits

Impudent Snobs

"A spirit of national masochism prevails, encouraged by an effete corps of impudent snobs who characterize themselves as intellectuals."

—Spiro Agnew (vice president, 1969–1973)

Inauguration

"Does that mean I have to get up?"

> —*Ronald Reagan, on the morning of his inauguration as President in 1981. His aide, Michael Deaver, said to him, "It's nine o'clock. You're going to be inaugurated in two hours."*

Insomnia

"The best cure for insomnia is to get a lot of sleep."

> —*S. I. Hayakawa (senator from California, 1977–1982)*

Internet

"The Internet is a great way to get on the Net."

> —*Bob Dole (1996 Republican presidential nominee)*

Intellectual Curiosity

"The state of California has no business subsidizing intellectual curiosity."

> —*Ronald Reagan, while governor of California, responding to student protests on college campuses*

Intimacy

"I got to be real intimate with people. Going into their living rooms and bedrooms, you know, seeing their underwear."

> —*Tom DeLay (representative from Texas, 1985–), describing his career as an exterminator*

Thomas Jefferson

"I didn't know Jefferson."

> —*Michael Huffington (representative from California, 1993–1994). Huffington had been asked if he admired Thomas Jefferson.*

Jews

"Oh, I've got too many of those now to hire you."

> —*William Scott (senator from Virginia, 1973–1978), after a prospective staff member told him she was Jewish*

Jobs

"I can do any one of your jobs as well as you, but I don't have the time."

> —*Phil Gramm (senator from Texas, 1985–), to his campaign staffers*

"I want to make sure everybody who has a job wants a job."

> —*George Bush*

Junkets

"This was not a junket in any sense of the word."

> *—Strom Thurmond (senator from South Carolina, 1954–).*
> *Thurmond took his wife, two children, eight staff members,*
> *and next-door neighbor on a five-day trip to the Paris Air*
> *Show—courtesy of the taxpayers.*

Jack Kemp

"Jack Kemp has probably showered with more blacks than most Republicans have shaken hands with."

> *—Newt Gingrich (Speaker, U.S. House of Representatives,*
> *1995–1998)*

Ted Kennedy

"I admire Ted Kennedy. How many fifty-nine-year-olds do you know who still go to Florida for spring break?"

> *—Pat Buchanan (1996 Republican presidential candidate)*

"I think any of us would be safer in a closet with David Souter than we would be in an automobile with Ted Kennedy."

> *—Rush Limbaugh (radio talk-show host)*

Language

"People said that my language was bad, but, Jesus—you should have heard LBJ!"

—*Richard Nixon*

Latin America

"Well, I learned a lot. . . . I went down [to Latin America] to find out from them and [learn] their views. You'd be surprised. They're all individual countries."

—*Ronald Reagan*

Law

"There has been much talk here this afternoon about the law of the land. We are the makers of the law of the land, and makers of the law of the land ought to understand and respect the law of the land."

—*Roger Jepsen (senator from Iowa, 1979–1985)*

"Goddamn it, forget the law."

—*Richard Nixon*

Legal System

"Mr. Haldeman has every right to be considered guilty until proven guilty"

> —*Richard Nixon, on his former chief of staff, Bob Haldeman*

Liberals

"I never use the words 'Democrats' and 'Republicans.' It's 'liberals' and 'Americans.'"

> —*James Watt (Secretary of the Interior, 1981–1983)*

"A friend of mine was asked to a costume ball a short time ago. He slapped some egg on his face and went as a liberal economist."

> —*Ronald Reagan*

Life

"Life is very important to Americans."

> —*Bob Dole (1996 Republican presidential nominee), asked if American lives were more important than foreign lives*

"Life is its own self, as Dan Jenkins said. Life is its own self. Figure that one out, Norm. But what it means is, I have a lot more to learn from President Reagan."

> —*George Bush*

"The loss of life will be irreplaceable."
—Dan Quayle, on the San Francisco earthquake in 1989

Abraham Lincoln

"If Lincoln were alive today, he'd roll over in his grave."
—Gerald Ford (president, 1974–1977)

Little People

"The little people have needs."
—Al D'Amato (senator from New York, 1981–1998), explaining why he was running for reelection

Love

"I didn't come to Washington to be loved, and I haven't been disappointed."
—Phil Gramm (senator from Texas, 1985–)

Loyalty

"I'm for Mr. Reagan—blindly."
—George Bush, while campaigning in 1984

"I would walk over my grandmother for Richard Nixon."
—Charles Colson (aide to President Nixon, 1969–1974)

"There's no difference between me and the president on taxes. No more nit-picking. Zip-ad-dee-doo-dah. Now it's off to the races!"

> —*George Bush, during the 1984 presidential campaign*

Lying

"Well, there was never a *Bible* in the room."

> —*William Clements (governor of Texas, 1979–1983), asked why he'd lied about approving payments to members of the Southern Methodist University football team*

Marriage

"Damnit, when you get married, you kind of expect you're going to get a little sex."

> —*Jeremiah Denton (senator from Alabama, 1981–1986). Denton had offered a bill to provide criminal immunity for raping a spouse.*

"You haven't thought about a new husband, have you?"

> —*Phil Gramm (senator from Texas, 1985–), responding to an elderly African-American widow who complained that his proposals to cut Social Security and Medicare would make it difficult for her to remain independent*

Mars

"Mars is essentially in the same orbit. Mars is somewhat the same distance from the sun, which is very important. We have seen pictures where there are canals, we believe, and water. If there is water, that means there is oxygen. If oxygen, that means we can breathe."

> —*Dan Quayle*

Mayors

"How are you, Mr. Mayor? I'm glad to meet you. How are things in your city?"

> —*Ronald Reagan, greeting Samuel Pierce, his Secretary of*
> *Housing and Urban Development, during a White House*
> *reception for mayors*

Mediocrity

"Even if he is mediocre, there are a lot of mediocre judges and lawyers. They are entitled to a little representation, aren't they, and a little chance? We can't have all Brandeises, Cardozos, and Frankfurters, and stuff like that there."

> —*Roman Hruska (senator from Nebraska, 1954–1976),*
> *defending President Nixon's nomination of G. Harrold Cars-*
> *well to the Supreme Court*

Mexican-Americans

"The little brown ones."

> —*George Bush, pointing out his three Mexican-American*
> *grandchildren to President Reagan during a 1988 campaign*
> *stop*

Middle Class

"When I see someone who is making anywhere from $300,000 to $750,000 a year, that's upper middle class."

> —*Fred Heineman (representative from North Carolina,*
> *1995–1996)*

Military

"As a twenty-six-year-old Ph.D. in economics I could have quit my job at A and M and joined the Army. I would have probably ended up working in some library or maybe teaching at West Point or working in the Pentagon. But I thought what I was doing at Texas A and M was important."

> —*Phil Gramm (senator from Texas, 1985–), explaining why he*
> *didn't serve in the military, despite his hawkish views*

"I went into the Air Force and volunteered for whatever dangerous assignment there was."

> —*Bob Dornan (representative from California, 1977–1983, 1985–1996). In fact, Dornan avoided action in Korea by going to drama school, and his subsequent military career was spent directing and performing in armed forces theatrical productions (though he did crash one helicopter and three jets while in training).*

"We have permitted our naval capability to deteriorate. At the same time, we are better off than we were a few years ago."

> —*Caspar Weinberger (Secretary of Defense, 1981–1988)*

"Wait a minute. I'm not interested in agriculture. I want the military stuff."

> —*William Scott (senator from Virginia, 1973–1978), being tutored by Pentagon generals about missile silos*

Minds

"What a waste it is to lose one's mind—or not to have a mind. How true that is."

> —*Dan Quayle, addressing representatives of the United Negro College Fund. He garbled their slogan, "A mind is a terrible thing to waste."*

Misstatements

"I stand by all the misstatements."

> —*Dan Quayle*

Mistakes

"I signed off on that wonderful transaction: Sammy Sosa for Harold Baines."

> —*George W. Bush (governor of Texas, 1995–), when asked in a debate to describe his biggest mistake as an adult*

Money

"My father once spent five million dollars on a birthday for himself in Tangiers. Why can't I spend a few more running for president?"

> —*Steve Forbes (2000 Republican presidential candidate)*

Monica

"I was Monica long before the other one was."

> —*Monica Monica (candidate for the U.S. House of Representatives from Louisiana, 1999)*

Murderers

"Obviously, when you see somebody go berserk and get a weapon and go in and murder people, of course, it troubles me."

> —*George Bush, after a gunman murdered twenty-three people in a Killeen, Texas, cafeteria*

Names

"General. I can't name the general. General."

> —*George W. Bush (governor of Texas, 1995–), asked by a reporter to name the leader of Pakistan*

NASA

"For NASA, space is still a high priority."

> —*Dan Quayle, speaking to NASA employees*

Negativism

"In the United States today, we have more than our share of the nattering nabobs of negativism."

> —*Spiro Agnew (vice president, 1969–1973). In 1970, Agnew also described Democrats as "pampered prodigies," "salons of sellout," and "pussilanimous pussyfooters."*

New Jersey

"There's a lot more to New Jersey than the Turnpike."

>*—Christine Todd Whitman (governor of New Jersey, 1994–), in a letter to Mitsubishi, demanding that it pull a commercial showing a car racing to escape odors on the New Jersey Turnpike*

Now Hear This

"I heard my words even when my lips weren't moving."

>*—Gary Bauer, 2000 Republican presidential hopeful after his last-place finish in the New Hampshire primary*

Nuclear Accidents

"It's too bad it didn't happen closer to the Kremlin."

>*—Steve Symms (senator from Idaho, 1981–1992), reacting to news of the 1986 Chernobyl accident*

"More people have died at Chappaquiddick than have died at nuclear power plants."

>*—Rush Limbaugh (radio talk-show host)*

"All the waste in a year from a nuclear power plant can be stored under a desk."

>*—Ronald Reagan*

Nutrition

"I strongly support the feeding of children."

>*—Gerald Ford (president, 1974–1977), while signing legislation
to fund school lunches*

Old MacDonald

"President Clinton had a bill, e-i-e-i-o. And in that bill was lots of pork, e-i-e-i-o."

>*—Al D'Amato (senator from New York, 1981–1998), singing
these lyrics on the floor of the Senate in 1994, criticizing
President Clinton's crime bill*

Panama Canal

"We should keep the Panama Canal. After all, we stole it fair and square."

>*—S. I. Hayakawa (senator from California, 1977–1982)*

Peanut Butter

"If you don't mind smelling like a peanut for two or three days, peanut butter is darn good shaving cream."

>*—Barry Goldwater (1964 Republican presidential nominee)*

Penises

"Do I let a group of powermongering men with short penises tell me what to do?"

> —*Doris Allen (California state representative, 1983–1995).*
> *Allen made this statement when she was Speaker of the California Assembly (which lasted three and a half months).*

Pessimism

"I mean, whine one, harvest moon!"

> —*George Bush, during his 1984 vice presidential debate with Geraldine Ferraro*

Pigtails

"I sure do like your pigtails."

> —*Clayton Williams (candidate for governor of Texas, 1990). A Native American responded, "This is a traditional hairstyle, and we call them braids." Williams said, "Well, I think your pigtails are real cute."*

Pledge of Allegiance

"I pledge allegiance to the flag of the United States of America, and to the Republicans for which it stands . . ."

> —*Bob McEwen (representative from Ohio, 1981–1992), as the U.S. House of Representatives opened its daily business*

Political Correctness

"Easter is displaced by Earth Day, Christmas becomes winter break, Columbus Day a day to reflect on the cultural imperialism and genocidal racism of the 'dead white males' who raped this continent while exterminating its noblest inhabitants."

—Pat Buchanan (1996 Republican presidential candidate)

Political Philosophy

"I want a government that does nothing."

—Michael Huffington (representative from California, 1993–1994)

Pollution

"Approximately 80 percent of our air pollution stems from hydrocarbons released by vegetation, so let's not go overboard in setting and enforcing tough emission standards from man-made sources."

—Ronald Reagan

"It isn't pollution that's harming the environment. It's the impurities in our air and water that are doing it."

—Dan Quayle

The Pope

"He no play-a da game, he no make-a da rules."

> —*Earl Butz (Secretary of Agriculture, 1971–1976), on the*
> *Pope's attitude toward birth control*

"I would have made a good pope."

> —*Richard Nixon*

Population Control

"Once America stood for freedom, liberty, and a Judeo-Christian moral order. Tomorrow in Cairo, the U.S. delegation will offer the world's poor IUDs, suction pumps, condoms, and Norplant."

> —*Pat Buchanan (1996 Republican presidential candidate),*
> *referring to the 1994 United Nations population conference*

Poverty

"We didn't do too well with the animal vote, did we? Isn't it the animals who live in these projects?"

> —*Al D'Amato (senator from New York, 1981–1998), explain-*
> *ing why he refused to help find funding for a low-income*
> *housing project in Brooklyn*

"We're the only nation in the world where all our poor people are fat."

> —*Phil Gramm (senator from Texas, 1985–)*

"The poor don't need gas because they're not working."

—S. I. Hayakawa (senator from California, 1977–1982)

Preparation

"One word sums up the responsibility of any vice president. And that word is 'to be prepared.'"

—Dan Quayle

Preservation

"This is Preservation Month. I appreciate preservations. It's what you do when you run for president. You gotta preserve."

—George W. Bush, speaking during "Perseverance Month" at Fairgrounds Elementary School in Nashua, New Hampshire

Progress

"Progression is not proclamation nor palaver. It is not pretense nor play on prejudice. It is not of personal pronouns, nor perennial pronouncement. It is not the perturbation of a people passion-wrought, nor a promise proposed."

—Warren G. Harding (president, 1921–1923)

Questions

"If the first witness answers 'Yes,' then ask him so and so. . . . If the witness answers 'No' or 'I'm not sure,' then ask him such and such."

> —*Strom Thurmond (senator from South Carolina, 1954–).*
> *Thurmond had read an opening statement at a congressional hearing—and then just kept on going. An aide rushed over to grab the paper from Thurmond.*

"But let me—I better switch over here for some more—and may I—a question—and I don't mean to offend with regard to follow-up—and I understand why you had them, but we've been reduced to the number of questions we get to ask when everybody has a follow-up. So ask them both at once."

> —*Ronald Reagan, during a 1984 press conference*

"The question we have to ask is: Is our children learning?"

> —*George W. Bush*

Racism

"Unfortunately, the people of Louisiana are not racists."

> —*Dan Quayle*

Nancy Reagan

"As a matter of fact, Nancy never had any interest in politics or anything else when we got married."

> —*Ronald Reagan*

Ronald Reagan

"Ronald Reagan doesn't dye his hair—he's just prematurely orange."

> —*Gerald Ford (president, 1974–1977)*

Reality

"If you're not in the *Washington Post* every day, you might as well not exist."

> —*Newt Gingrich (Speaker, U.S. House of Representatives, 1995–1998)*

"Things are more like they are now than they have ever been."
> —*Gerald Ford (president, 1974–1977)*

Relaxation

"I've got to run now and relax. The doctor told me to relax. The doctor told me. He was the one. He said, 'Relax.'"

> —*George Bush, during a 1991 press conference*

Religion

"No, thanks. Once was enough."

> —*William Clements (governor of Texas, 1979–1983), asked if he had been "born again."*

Republican Party

"We are America. Those other people are not."

> *—Rich Bond (chairman, Republican National Committee, 1992–1993), referring to protesters at the 1992 Republican National Convention*

"One of the great problems in the Republican Party is that we don't encourage you to be nasty."

> *—Newt Gingrich (Speaker, U.S. House of Representatives, 1995–1998), in a 1978 speech to College Republicans in Atlanta*

Revolutions

"Leading a revolution means more than borrowing a bottle of Grecian Formula."

> *—Arianna Huffington (syndicated columnist), referring to Bob Dole*

Right Wing

"He's in the right wing of the Capitol. But to get there you gotta take a right, then you take another far right, and then you go to the extreme right, and he should be right there."

> *—Bob Dole (1996 Republican presidential nominee), helping the* Tonight Show *staff find Congressman Sonny Bono's office*

Righteousness

"My friends, no matter how rough the road may be, we can and we will never, never surrender to what is right."

> —*Dan Quayle, telling the Christian Coalition that abstinence was the best way to avoid AIDS*

Rock and Roll

"The Nitty Ditty Nitty Gritty Great Bird."

> —*George Bush, at a country music awards ceremony in Nashville, attempting to refer to the Nitty Gritty Dirt Band*

Rural America

"It's rural America. It's where I came from. We always refer to ourselves as real America. Rural America, real America, real, real America."

> —*Dan Quayle*

Saving Money

"Eat less."

> —*Robert A. Taft (senator from Ohio, 1938–1953), advising housewives how to save money*

Scandal

"Well, I was raised a Democrat."

—Jerry Falwell (president, Moral Majority, 1979–1990), asked if he had any skeletons in his closet

Scholarship

"I was a less-than-serious student in college. If I had it to do over again, I would be far more serious. I did play a lot of golf. But I don't think that's any reflection on my ability to lead this nation."

—Dan Quayle

School Prayer

"Most people don't realize it's illegal to pray in public schools."

—Newt Gingrich (Speaker, U.S. House of Representatives, 1995–1998)

Senate

"The bottom line is there have been a lot of nuts elected to the United States Senate."

—Charles Grassley (senator from Iowa, 1981–), explaining why Republicans shouldn't be upset about Oliver North running for the Senate

"There are a lot of things that we do that are irrelevant, but that's what the Senate is for."

> —*Alan Simpson (senator from Wyoming, 1979–1996)*

Sex

"Well, David, did you do any fornicating this weekend?"

> —*Richard Nixon, to television host David Frost*

"It was a lot different then in those days. The houses were the only places you got serviced then."

> —*Clayton Williams (candidate for governor of Texas, 1990). In 1990, a rumor began that Williams rewarded his top employees with "honey hunts." Reportedly, Williams would hire a bunch of prostitutes and then take everyone to his ranch and let his boys have their way.*

"For seven and a half years I've worked alongside President Reagan. We've had triumphs. Made some mistakes. We had some sex . . . uh . . . setbacks."

> —*George Bush*

"Suddenly the pouting sex kitten gave way to Diana the Huntress. She rolled onto him and somehow was sitting athwart his chest, her knees pinning his shoulders. 'Tell me, or I will do terrible things,' she hissed."

> —*Newt Gingrich (Speaker, U.S. House of Representatives, 1995–1998). This is from the first draft of Newt's novel, 1945.*

Sexual Harassment

"Sexual harassment on the job is not a problem for virtuous women."

—*Phyllis Schlafly (founder, Eagle Forum)*

Sluggish Times

"We're enjoying sluggish times, and we're not enjoying them very much."

—*George Bush*

Slums

"I didn't say I wouldn't go into ghetto areas. I've been in many of them and to some extent I would say this: If you've seen one city slum, you've seen them all."

—*Spiro Agnew (vice president, 1969–1973)*

Sobriety

"I stay in enough trouble when I'm sober."

—*Tommy Robinson (candidate for governor of Arkansas, 1990), asked about rumors that he used to consume a pint of bourbon every day*

Soviet Union

"My fellow Americans. I'm pleased to announce that I've signed legislation outlawing the Soviet Union. We begin bombing in five minutes."

> —*Ronald Reagan, telling a "joke" during a radio mike check before his regular Saturday radio broadcast on August 12, 1984*

Space

"I believe space tourism will be a common fact of life during the adulthood of children born this year, that honeymoons in space will be the vogue by 2020. Imagine weightlessness and its effects and you will understand some of the attractions."

> —*Newt Gingrich (Speaker, U.S. House of Representatives, 1995–1998)*

"Space is almost infinite. As a matter of fact, we think it is infinite."

> —*Dan Quayle, head of the Space Council in the Bush administration*

Space Aliens

"It's mathematically plausible."

> —*Newt Gingrich (Speaker, U.S. House of Representatives, 1995–1998)*

Speeches

"When a man is asked to make a speech, the first thing he has to decide is what to say."

> —*Gerald Ford (president, 1974–1977)*

Spelling

"If Al Gore invented the Internet, I invented spellcheck."

> —*Dan Quayle*

"It's an easy name to spell. Only five letters."

> —*Charles Colson (Nixon White House aide), explaining why his name appeared so frequently in Watergate testimony*

Sports

"I love sports. Whenever I can, I always watch the Detroit Tigers on radio."

> —*Gerald Ford (president, 1974–1977)*

Strategy

"Bobby Knight told me, 'There is nothing that a good defense cannot beat a better offense.' In other words, a good offense wins."

> —*Dan Quayle*

Student Loans

"Well, I wouldn't have been able to go to school if I didn't have a student loan."

> —*Jon Christensen (representative from Nebraska, 1995–1997). During a Nebraska radio interview, Congressman Christensen energetically attacked welfare recipients, saying he favored reducing all government "handouts and subsidies" to "eliminate people's reliance on government." The host then pointed out that Christensen had outstanding student loans of between $30,000 and $100,000.*

Target Prices

"Target prices? How that works? I know quite a bit about farm policy. I come from Indiana, which is a farm state. Deficiency payments—which are the key—that is what gets money into the farmers' hands. We got loan, uh, rates, we got target, uh, prices, uh, I have worked very close with my senior colleague, Richard Lugar, making sure that the farmers of Indiana are taken care of."

> —*Dan Quayle*

Tax Dollars

"Your tax dollars are being used to pay for grade-school classes that teach our children that cannibalism, wife-swapping, and the murder of infants and the elderly are acceptable behavior."

—Jesse Helms (senator from North Carolina, 1973–), in a 1981 fund-raising letter for the National Conservative Political Action Committee

Teachers

"Quite frankly, teachers are the only profession that teaches our children."

—Dan Quayle

Teen Pregnancy

"Statistics show that teen pregnancy drops off significantly after age 25."

—Mary Anne Tebedo (Colorado state senator, 1989–)

Teletubbies

"He is purple—the gay pride color; and his antenna is shaped like a triangle—the gay pride symbol."

—Jerry Falwell (president, Moral Majority, 1979–1990). Falwell issued a "parent alert" in his National Liberty Journal *that Tinky Winky, a character in the TV show* Teletubbies, *is gay.*

Term Limits

"I support efforts to limit the terms of members of Congress, especially members of the House and members of the Senate."

> *—Dan Quayle*

"It's an obvious inconsistency. That I admit. I have no defense."

> *—Bob Inglis (representative from South Carolina, 1993–1998),*
> *a term limits supporter, on his endorsement of forty-year*
> *incumbent Senator Strom Thurmond*

Them

"When I was coming up, it was a dangerous world, but we knew exactly who the "they" were. It was us versus them. . . . Today we're not so sure who they are, but we know they're there."

> *—George W. Bush, governor of Texas, on post–Cold War*
> *politics*

Tobacco

"I was with some Vietnamese recently, and some of them were smoking two cigarettes at a time. That's the kind of customers we need!"

> *—Jesse Helms (senator from North Carolina, 1973–), on his*
> *meeting with the Vietnamese ambassador-designate at a*
> *dinner given by the R. J. Reynolds Company*

Trees

"A tree is a tree. How many more do you need to look at?"
> —*Ronald Reagan, declaring his opposition in 1966 to the expansion of Redwoods Park in California*

"Trees cause more pollution than automobiles."
> —*Ronald Reagan*

Trends

"I believe we are on an irreversible trend toward more freedom and democracy. But that could change."
> —*Dan Quayle*

Undecided Voters

"It's no exaggeration to say the undecideds could go one way or another."
> —*George Bush, during a 1988 campaign rally in Troy, Ohio*

Unemployment

"When more and more people are thrown out of work, unemployment results."
> —*Calvin Coolidge (president, 1923–1929)*

"We are trying to get unemployment to go up, and I think we're going to succeed."
> —*Ronald Reagan*

Unions

"I believe in unions and I believe in non-unions."

—*George Bush*

Verbosity

"I just am not one who—who flamboyantly believes in throwing a lot of words around."

—*George Bush*

"Verbosity leads to unclear, inarticulate things."

—*Dan Quayle*

Vice Presidency

"I'm the Vice President. They know it, and they know that I know it."

—*Dan Quayle*

Vietnam

"I could have ended the war in a month. I could have made North Vietnam look like a mud puddle."

—*Barry Goldwater (1964 Republican presidential nominee)*

"It was not a bombing of Cambodia. It was a bombing of North Vietnam in Cambodia."

—*Henry Kissinger (Secretary of State, 1971–1976)*

Violence

"It is the most exciting thing since my tenth birthday, when I rode a roller coaster for the first time."

> —S. I. Hayakawa (senator from California, 1977–1982). At the time, Hayakawa was president of San Francisco State University, where nine antiwar protesters were killed.

Vision

"Oh, the vision thing."

> —George Bush, responding to a friend's suggestion that he go to Camp David to figure out his themes for the 1992 presidential campaign

Voting

"Vote early, and then vote often. That's what we do in Texas."

> —Barbara Bush, campaigning in 1998 for her son, Jeb Bush, who was elected governor of Florida

"Now, Prop 1 is which, excuse me?"

> —Clayton Williams (candidate for governor of Texas, 1990), when asked how he had voted on the only proposition on the Texas ballot in 1990

Wake-up Calls

"I have left orders to be awakened at any time in case of national emergency—even if I'm in a Cabinet meeting."

> —*Ronald Reagan*

Watergate

"What was Watergate? A little bugging!"

> —*Richard Nixon (president, 1969–1974)*

"Nobody drowned at Watergate."

> —*Earl Butz (Secretary of Agriculture, 1971–1976)*

"I was not lying. I said things that later on seemed to be untrue."

> —*Richard Nixon (president, 1969–1974), in a 1978 television interview with David Frost*

"Well, we got the burglar vote."

> —*Bob Dole (1996 Republican presidential nominee). In 1973, Dole was chairman of the Republican National Committee. He was asked how the Watergate affair would affect GOP prospects at the polls.*

Weather

"The warm-climate community just hasn't found the colder climate that attractive. It's an area of America that simply has never attracted the Afro-American or the Hispanic."

> —*Helen Chenoweth (representative from Idaho, 1995–), arguing that the U.S. Forest Service shouldn't bother to recruit racial minorities to Idaho*

Weirdness

"People that are really weird can get into sensitive positions and have a tremendous impact on history."

> —*Dan Quayle*

Welfare State

"The welfare state kills more people in a year than private business."

> —*Newt Gingrich (Speaker, U.S. House of Representatives, 1995–1998)*

Lawrence Welk

"I'm for Lawrence Welk. Lawrence Welk is a wonderful man. He used to be, or was—or wherever he is now, bless him."

> —*George Bush*

White House Drug Dealers

"Now, like, I'm President. It would be pretty hard for some drug guy to come into the White House and start offering it up, you know? . . . I bet if they did, I hope I would say, 'Hey, get lost. We don't want any of that.'"

> —*George Bush, speaking to a group of students about drug abuse at the White House*

Women

"Sophia Loren is not a citizen."

> —*Phil Gramm (senator from Texas, 1985–). Gramm was asked in 1996 if he might choose a woman as his vice presidential running mate.*

"I want to turn women loose on the environmental crisis. . . . Nobody knows more about pollution when detergents back up in the kitchen sink."

> —*Nelson Rockefeller (vice president, 1974–1977)*

"There are so many women on the floor of Congress, it looks like a mall."

> —*Henry Hyde (representative from Illinois, 1975–)*

"Female militants are more of an object of ridicule and a pain in the butt than the black chauvinists."

> —*Pat Buchanan (1996 Republican presidential candidate)*

"If it wasn't for women, us men would still be walking around in skin suits carrying clubs."

—*Ronald Reagan, addressing a women's group*

"Women are hard enough to handle now without giving them a gun."

—*Barry Goldwater (1964 Republican presidential nominee), on women in the armed services*

Yes-Men

"The President doesn't want any yes-men and yes-women around him. When he says no, we all say no."

—*Elizabeth Dole (2000 presidential candidate), referring to President Reagan. At the time, Dole was on Reagan's White House staff.*

Youth

"Youth lacks, to some extent, experience."

—*Spiro Agnew (vice president, 1969–1973)*